Lake Effect
Country

Lake Effect Country

Poems

A. R. AMMONS

W · W · NORTON & COMPANY

NEW YORK   LONDON

Copyright © 1983 by A. R. Ammons
All rights reserved.
Published simultaneously in Canada by George J. McLeod Limited, Toronto.
Printed in the United States of America.

The text of this book is composed in Janson.
Manufacturing by The Maple-Vail Book Manufacturing Group.

FIRST EDITION

Library of Congress Cataloging in Publication Data
Ammons, A. R., 1926–
Lake effect country: Poems
I. Title.
PS3501.M6L3   1983   811'.54   82–10601

ISBN 0-393-01702-8
ISBN 0-393-30104-4 (pbk.)

W. W. Norton & Company, Inc., 500 Fifth Avenue, New York, N.Y. 10110
W. W. Norton & Company Ltd., 37 Great Russell Street, London WC1B 3NU

1 2 3 4 5 6 7 8 9 0

Acknowledgments

Many thanks to the editors of the following instruments for first publishing the poems listed:

The American Scholar
  "Negative Pluses"
Grapevine
  "Songlet"
The Green River Review
  "Zero and Then Some"
The Hudson Review
  "By the Boulder Cluster the Wind"
The Manhattan Review
  "The Fairly High Assimilation Rag"
  "The Spiral Rag"
Palaemon Press Limited
  first published "Dusk Water" as a broadside
Pembroke Magazine
  "Nature Poetry"
Poetry
  "Meeting Place"
  "Singling & Doubling Together"
  "Yadkin Picnic"
The Poetry Miscellany
  "Localizing"
  "Retiring"
Ubu
  "I Could not be Here at All"

for Edwin G. Wilson
friend's friend

Contents

Lake Effect
Country

The Bright Side

Bliss is the
trace of
existence that
persists in
the idea of
nothingness—

thinking
nothingness
is a presence
fragile as
the longing look
through

tragedy, the
frail whirl
the mind climbs
(the defense
against
absolute beginnings

or endings)
the inward-turning
edge of
the outermost,
the light that sets
in the utterly empty eye.

Zero and Then Some

We would not want to persuade ourselves
on eternity with an insistence of
our own, pre-empting narrowly or

warping out of centrality the nature of what is—
nevertheless we would not want to miss a
right praising, even if we had to reduce

the praise from substance and stand empty
in stance alone, an attitude merely or
willingness that would at least shirk

indifference in wanting not to avoid praise:
whatever forever is we would not want to be
unconjoined with it or only in the ways

the temporal and particular necessarily
fall short of staying put: there is
an ongoing we nearly cheapen by being its

specific crest, but humbly we know too it
bore us and will support us into whatever
rest remains: what if the infinite

filters through here ordinary as if it
were just taking place locally? that is,
though the infinite is quite impressive

it may be like a weak gravity field, the
least spectacular thing around, the
immediate's most trifling ingredient: we

probably couldn't detect it to redress or
address it, amass it to praise it, not with
regular human instrumentation: but addle

us enough, we will drop the whole
subject and invent for substitution "that
which is to be praised" and invest it with

our store of verve, no matter: the jay
will sometimes at dawn sit in the blue spruce
as if too blank to stir first and

piddle idly in song like a swinging
squeak or singing wheel: it could be praise
though how it works or why it's sung, we guess.

Localizing

The ground that life's unpredictability
dissolves is possibility's very furrow,
the frail white root letting down

or unfolding into mix's raw mush, loam:
the doubleness, not necessarily two things
but of one thing being two: the pivot that

could skew either way: imbalance, though,
balances imbalance, there's a pure category,
and new rudeness ameliorates old ruin:

God's will (the Way) everybody knows holds
grave assimilations of constancy in change,
that constancy though probably too high out

of things for any but undifferentiated effect:
and then the effect is as if from underneath!
well, it's nice to know that even

broaching error you may get something right,
or that not knowing sometimes finds a
better than known road, although in the

long run everything wilts down and withers
over, undone as beached seaweed: if we step
forward, it is into the shambles of our

time to come; and whether we step forward
or not, we are forwarded daily to a sparer
dimension, lessened mansion: but surely

there is a Will so high change can't stir
it nor loss nor gain stagger it, spirit
unshadowed and shadowless! but we love it here!

Theories of Height

Scaling the tiers of dominance,
one obliterates categories,
level by shrinking level,
till one,

in the highest golden room,
turns about alone,
floating, disconnected, all
the world won,

perished beneath one's sight, no equal to
be addressed by and no
one to address: whereas, the meek,
in this

case the emotion wherever it
abide and the people,
do, indeed, with no fights,
inherit

the earth, the whole
range, the humblest
sweets and asides,
and the only solid view of height.

The Spiral Rag

Opposites attracting could easing jar to a standstill
or unmoderated blast into mutual annihilation's O; or,
just at the meeting node, veer around each other,

the momentum transforming into spin which would, of
course, generate a whirlpool flow-through, so that the
energies undemolished and still current could find a

place where, slowed, they could give up their terrible
shapes and tendencies and dissipate into the continuum
from which they might eventually return: anyway, the

circle won't do, except as an infinitely extensible outer
boundary: also, the sphere won't do, for some reason
I've forgotten (no transfusing discharge) just surface

extension with only surface flow: but the vortex will
come close to doing because it gives a standing-motion
shape at the central interior so that high formations

finding each other have a way to go: the truest motion's
truest shape's the spiral's inward arc, the inward
turning whirl that promotes a direction for the

meeting that can wear down or fly apart somewhere past
the tightening screw's whirl: whatever, what
a mechanism for averting, for taking in, changing, and

giving out, for holding still while the motion flies!
the mind figures but even though it wants to do well
never comes up with the source of what it comes up with.

The Fairly High Assimilation Rag

Plato derives the many from the one and Aristotle
the one from the many, and these two together give
the flip-flop sides of a dynamics too

one and two for easy entry or exit: parallel with
that philosophical goes the religious, in which
the One devolves and assuages into the fiats and

specifications of specialized deities, into poly-
theism, and in which the many accumulate up, dissolving
their intense boundaries into the blurs and glows

and finally on up of course to the absolute absence
and clarity of the total presence, One unspeakable,
monotheism: answering back and forth with heat

exchangers and mitochondria and other particulars in
and out of focus is the hierarchy, the one:many
mechanism we everywhere seek and renounce: like

a mobile in which the wires are, though the only
means of support, hardly visible and where the bright
parts at liberty to play seem to be the reason for it all—

like that we seek the rigorous, tense, thin dispositions
that allow the colorful personal feelings of free,
unoriented, singular family, all the way to the play

out of each his individual set of bones and wishes:
oh yes: the one:many's the metaphysical (and discrete)
wherein we entertain systems high and low, sharp and

fuzzy, radiant and drained, pertaining to most anything:
still, we don't look to the wiring for immediate
help or hope as often as to the family vacations,

and we are hurt by nothing so much as children's
chances, their terrible uprisings and misleading
procedures: society will wind and unwind but we may

or may not have a nice weekend depending on whether
or not we have been divorced or have enough booze
to last through Sunday: the particulars are so

close they are nobody else's business (largely)
whereas everybody does a little for the hierarchy
without which we would not know which way to turn.

I Could Not Be Here At All

Momentous and trivial, I
walk along the lake cliff
and look north where the lake
curls to a wisp through the hills

and say as if to the lake,
I'm here, too,
and to the winter storm centered
gnarl-black over the west bank,

I nearly call out, it's me, I'm here:
the wind-fined
snow nicks
my face, mists my lashes

and the sun, not dwindling me, goes
on down behind the storm and the reed
withes' wind doesn't whistle, brother! brother!
and no person comes.

Written Water

I hope I will go through
the period of hunger
for immortality and be stated—
so that I can rise

at last from that death into communion with
things, the flowing free of
grave trenches in rain, the
indifferent and suitable toppling

of stones, the wiping out of
borders and prints, stains, inks;
so that I can abide the
rinse of change as the fountainhead's

coolest, freshest drink, the
immortality likeliest to last, the clarity
whose clarion no decay smuts,
change's pure arising in constant souls

Retiring

I'll keep the brook watched,
the crinkles of light
between flow-stones
bundled into sheaves:

I'll sort the clouds into
categories between
the great names—
nimbostratus, cirrocumulus—

till so many fine distinctions
become clouds again:
I'll probably get the sun
up and down, turn

the stars through the round
sprinkling sheets, become essential
at all the wind's swerves,
keeping it going right.

Nature Poetry

If no one sends you
messages to read, none
you can read
(so you have no
replies to shape)
still you may irrelevantly read

messages sent to
no one, light shaking
off a poplar leaf
(like seen wind chipped free)
or breaking into
threads

of bright-backed water
in brookstone shallows:
these
messages, though
not sent to you and
requiring no response

may nevertheless be
taken
down in strict
observances (like studied regard)
as if to be nearly adequate
messages to no one.

Holding Still

A whirlwind held still
in the sideyard this
afternoon
a minute, three
or four of last
year's leaves,
one split and one
with a lobe ripped off,
caught up:
I thought the leaves
at first astonishing
butterflies, hardly
enough figures there to
point a whirlwind's
center and
traveling: but soon
the structure broke
away, its currents
wobbling
out of the wound-up winding:
the leaves scooted
up remnant loops
and fell out randomly
about, still—
the eye of the hop-wobbly
baby rabbit, crouched
nearby under the small
pine, still, with a
whirlwind in it.

Windy Morning with a Little Sleet

The roar of the wind coming
gets here before the wind

doing sixty does and the airy
billows sizzling fry rolling

uphill from the lake till
tugging and tearing they

fall on our flat walls and poor
bushes: I wish we had left

the trees on this continent
up, but then there would have

been too many wolves and timber
rattlers: still, the streams

would have been as constant
and clear as diamonds, and

the wind probably would have
been as soft as *bough* sounds:

poor shrubs & bushes, scant
borders of ice-slick fields,

what a scraggly fringe you make
against this stripped harrowing,

the naked wind, where once in
the cathedral of trees the

turrets would have stirred only
to bedazzle bits of
sunlight on the prayer-still floor.

Playback

After the inch-deep
snowfall around midnight
(spring arriving at
12:03) the clouds
cleared out and the
clarion full moon
(full moon & equinox
coming together splitting
reality open)
lit the lawn
brilliant, and the rabbits
romped under &
around the big spruce
(I saw it this morning)
the clumps of prints
coming and going
& here and there entangling,
dispute for
territory or sexual rights,
or love itself
irresponsible between two,
or the plain
evenness of fullness—
the moon, the balanced day
and night, amplitude
for the emergence of
a time well taken.

Positive Edges

As glimmer goes
off dusk
water

the spirit frees
itself from
shapes,

no gain to the
spirit world,
already filled, and

no loss among the
shapes,
the subtraction netting

nothing, where
addition had lolloped
all day,

splintered into white
spray or
flattened tremor-brilliant:

with one, play and
plenty: with the other,
nothing missing.

On Being

The one who wishes
to be
loves definition

that clearly announces
to the other
things that are

shapely assertion
but the one
who cringes to be

what he is
twists wrestling
with the arrival

of hateful exactitude
and the clear
pointing out

of limited difference
till throwing
away

the lines, halters,
blinds of
dense body,

he throws away
the city, country,
earth itself

and finds no
place to gentle
down till

(the soft land where
the jostle is slow
and surmise hazy)

nothingness's
wide amplitude
makes his place

By the Boulder Cluster the Wind

By the boulder cluster the wind
struck up a dust-ghost,
a brothering shade and shadow,
and oh I said
that I could live lively as you
and have
no more to die

and the ghost tore
into a shackling shrub
and failed like sleet,
returning
shape's interference
to clearing.

The dust rearranging
to a new breeze
I gave up
the intermediate
paradise
and said so
all things do from misty arisings
mistily depart,
shingling down
the rills and ruffles
of nothing-in-between.

Instancing

Foolish of course to spend
time with sticks &
rocks & spindly shifts

of weeds, say things to them,
and make them say things back:
glows hide

still to be named in human
faces, studied, tones speech
can't surface responded to:

but should one who has
no ticket to feasts be harmed
if he banquets on

a crumb or marvels a bit
of cheese into plenty: leave
him to the coined riches

at least should one of those at
table lose his place and need
quick tips on dining on nothing alone.

Trigger

I almost step on
a huge spider:
it stalls and
disperses
like oil-beads on water,
baby spiders
shedding radially
till a skinny
mother hardly
shades the
spent center.

Apologetics

I don't amount to a thing, I said to the mountain:
I'm not worth a tuft of rubble: I come from
nothing, that's where I'll go: you take, like, from

my elevation, everything rises, slopes with huge
shoulders barreling and breaking up as if out of
melt-deep ground: when I look out I don't see

a scope falling away under prevailing views
into ridges, windings, plots, stream-fields: sir,
the mountain noticing me below and fixing

me in view said, what you don't have you nearly
acquire in the telling, there is a weaving
winding round in you lifting you buzzardlike up into

high-windings: just a minute, I said to the
mountain: exaggeration is not your prerogative:
you have to settle for size: eminence is mine.

Songlet

Death, unduly undoing,
kisses us awake into
the new world and leaves

us pre-empted and unsteady:
oh, here we go, we say,
another adjustment as usual:

light appears to be the leader
here: we turn to where
a beam forms and set out

Is the Only Enough None

If to my nuzzlings &
whimpers for meaning
rapids stopped to

break open their going—
or if to my eyes'
rolling for filling

light the fringes of
lit clouds congealed
to gold or if

my loose mind waited
by the glacier
for the core-stream

to shine in thaw—
I would be rather put
out at getting things

right or rather when
meaningful and held
I finally considered

matters through, then
motion's shows might
recommence leaving my

hordes emptiness but
me, then, light enough
to get back in the act

Giving up Word with Words

Isn't it time to let things be:
I don't pick up the drafts-book,
I ease out of the typewriter room:

bumblebees' wings swirl
free of the fine-spun of words:
the brook blinks

a leaf down-bed, shadow mingling,
tumbling with the leaf, with no
help from me: do things let alone

go to pieces: is rescue written
already into the motions of coherence:
have words all along

imitated work better done undone:
one thinks not ruthlessly to bestir again:
one eases off harsh attentions

to watch the dew dry, the squirrel stand
(white belly prairie-dog erect)
the mayfly cling daylong to the doorscreen.

Settling Up

I think my
light won't
slow down
to matter,
my wind be
air to any
thicket,
my stream bend
round
to any dam
and yet light,
wind, stream
help me
find
the eyes in whose
library I
read lasting scriptures

Negative Pluses

One whose impulses are
received, encouraged
by the world finds
a place to put down cool,
settle: one who when
he touches down feels the
burn of difference,
exclusion must
like a hoped-for fusion
system
suspend his reactions
midair: this involves
centering radially
many sides, a skinless air mass
that drops down
and bounds up again
risking loops
gravity might not recover from:
one in this wise
develops rotundity of preparation
and defense, an undue
awareness of transience,
and a sense of place complex
enough to represent reality
and simple enough
to be profoundly clear.

Yadkin Picnic

for Jane and Pat Kelly

It takes so long to set up the terminological landscape,
a rise of assimilation here, wooded underpinnings
fringed by thickets of possibility there, and throughout

in a slope, an undulation falling away to one side, an
old river's work—before one can say, "May we sweetly
kiss" or "Mark, the woodlark"—:   begins with an airy

nothingness lofted, on one arc of which is a great sea and in
the middle of the sea an island, in the middle of which
a city, and mid-city a spire, the coming to point

of the tallest assumption: after this, it follows
naturally to say, "Yesterday, after the morning clouds, we
packed lunch and went over to picnic in Aunt Polly's orchard."

Laces

I've been around
practically anything
you can mention
(twice)
and spring, elation's
bump, has come
more than once:
seed
cut loose from the elm's
windy height have grown
elm's elsewhere:
ends have tied and untied
but the knot of ourselves
unwinds once

The Only Way Around Is Through

I've lost my ambition to be somebody:
what is there to be except
free of the need to be somebody:

the brook doesn't save itself: slate
honings, root wear, underminings,
silt-flow slopes

express to the sweetest reader former
times and ways but
the brook isn't trying mainly to stay recalled:

enough remains, bits, bunches, not to
take currency out of change: but
the brook's glassy noise this

evening (jay and robin fighting dominion
out in a bankside crabapple bush)
feels like its oldest recollection, the song

brassy, ledge-displaced, ledge-displayed
rattle-rush hard to find anything to to
repeat yet always the same: trying to

write free of writing keeps me
at it, writing my brook, not
to keep but to mumble by with.

Old Desire

I wake up around three or four these mornings
and lie awake
in a region fine as a door ajar between
sleep and waking
and burn cold about death, near and unfamiliar,
first for half an hour,
and then burn for fifteen minutes over the
clowning that was the day past:

burning turns to desire, the
thrashing, and my passions,
late-polished, light up memories of
old passions also bright and, though spent, still
not spent
and then, fire considered into coals,
I drift at length into furrows of doze and
wake to light coming, geese calling—

but this morning I saw on my walk
a squeaky bunch of tiny birds
light out, high leaping, into the high northwind,
from one tree
and fly (swerving, bounding) half a mile of air
a hundred yards to the next reef of boughs:
so much for me for ever springing
out and touching down in desire again.

Making Room

I will not have
what I desire

for that
would unwind me,

but not to have
what I desire

is a near
unwinding:

I move
then

in a deserted
edge

till the abundance I
desire,

starved out, becomes
this abundant space

Exchangers

The spruce bough looks so cold
and stiff and then the creaking
wind picks up as if to dash

motion into splinters and
smithereens: the crows, addled
with no place to put down, lurch

at least from branch to branch,
spilling some snow, or surge
deeply down to cast off into

flight, burdens of snow then
coming undone, the
branch whipping up flexible

again into loadlessness,
black crow-weight to be borne any time
for such springy reprieves from white

Lips Twisted with Thirst

Lips twisted with thirst
in the hot country
I came to the glacial stream
and drank earnestly
as men frame desire
and said
   what reservoir, bowl then
lifted by sphinx-implicit stone
to the falcon air
has the soul from drought
   I took off the garment of flesh
   unhinged the beams of my liquid day
and watched my desert-precious being
swim, wily as snake-water in the sand
   Unused to winds
   liberated to rejected light
the soul cowered in its final sheath of wings
and turning from the naked dignity
and cracking drought
I spoke in the presence of it
   Tree cones and clouds
retold the unknown tongue
and heralds from the sun came
bearing my message
to my scrawny soul

The Eclipse Goes By Drawing

The eclipse goes by drawing
the moon-blood out
cleansing our shadow
from too much
familiarity so
let us resolve to make an affirmation
casually at first but then

going a long way about
so that arriving we shall not know
how to return:
you sit as in rain
one arm across the knees
and the other falling with a nut
to the squirrel

and you stand naked with a bow
full in sunlight
one hound leaping perhaps and
you try
to be leafy
while these two
below

will be conversant but
with only a little motion:
surely when we have brought this off
and settled down for usual
no one will
be ruthless
and shrug out of it.

Dusk Water

Looks like, the rain run off, the brook's
pane-deep again and
over the flat shale-squares
hardly blurs to move:

bushes overhang (small trout floating
leaf-still in hollows) but
I can see when
the catbird lights in, his skinny

feet cracking the mirror,
and then follows so much
shattering and splinter-flicking! which
though when he

stops wet to look around,
melts back, all the rag
beads and quivers and the small mist,
to double-bird fine glass.

Pet Panther

My attention is a wild
animal: it will if idle
make trouble where there
was no harm: it will

sniff and scratch at the
breath's sills:
it will wind itself tight
around the pulse

or, undistracted by
verbal toys, pommel the
heart frantic: it will
pounce on a stalled riddle

and wrestle the mind numb:
attention, fierce animal,
I cry, as it coughs in my
face, dislodges boulders

in my belly, lie down, be
still, have mercy, here
is song, coils of song, play
it out, run with it.

Singing & Doubling Together

My nature singing in me is your nature singing:
you have means to veer down, filter through,
and, coming in,
harden into vines that break back with leaves,
so that when the wind stirs
I know you are there and I hear you in leafspeech,

though of course back into your heightenings I
can never follow: you are there beyond
tracings flesh can take,
and farther away surrounding and informing the systems,
you are as if nothing, and
where you are least knowable I celebrate you most

or here most when near dusk the pheasant squawks and
lofts at a sharp angle to the roost cedar,
I catch in the angle of that ascent,
in the justness of that event your pheasant nature,
and when dusk settles, the bushes creak and
snap in their natures with your creaking

and snapping nature: I catch the impact and turn
it back: cut the grass and pick up branches
under the elm, rise to the several tendernesses
and griefs, and you will fail me only as from the still
of your great high otherness you fail all things,
somewhere to lift things up, if not those things again:

even you risked all the way into the taking on of shape
and time fail and fail with me, as me,
and going hence with me know the going hence
and in the cries of that pain it is you crying and
you know of it and it is my pain, my tears, my loss—
what but grace

have I to bear in every motion,
embracing or turning away, staggering or standing still,
while your settled kingdom sways in the distillations of light
and plunders down into the darkness with me
and comes nowhere up again but changed into your
singing nature when I need sing my nature nevermore.

Motioning

My father did not
get a resolution
to his problems: he

was taken down
from them: a
vessel broke

in his brain, and
he lost half his
capability: he

walked less and
asked no questions:
sense returned

to his eyes and
with one hand he held
the other

up: that was
stopped when the
central

heart, of which there
is only one,
ticked off: my

father, I could
tell, had
a lot of questions to

ask: but all
motion was
removed from the matter.

Love's Motions

The old woman, toothless
as an infant, rocked
back and forth slowly

on the cot, figuring
outwardly the binds she
had come to, but smiled,

hassling, at the son-in-law,
stuffed hard-fat in the
corner chair, his mouth

breezy with superhighways,
tunnels, interchanges,
the grayed daughter

obviously concerned but
chipping in about the
cloverleaves and the hard

kids left behind: the doctor
came in, sat down beside
the old woman, and took

her hand to count: she
looked at him and calm
and new confidence came

over her: the doctor said,
"Here, try this walker:"
the old woman stood up and

nudging forward held on with
both hands: "Look a there,"
she said, "wonder if
I'll ever learn to walk."

Helping Hand

They told Miss Lou
it was her heart:
she said somehow I

didn't think it
was my heart—
but went on

believing them when
the colon
was removed and

while her skin sheered
several shades
of white

till they rushed her
pure white away for
blood and then she

thought maybe it was her
heart for the pints
of sudden blood

troubled and stopped
it: she
called help, help,

the assault crumbling,
sheets of dark warping
past her: hold me,

she cried, not against
going down but
to steady her through.

Debris

Say something and then
question it nearly
out of existence: or split

something cleanly down
the middle, but make
one side as if

wrestle and beg for
the opposites and complements
of the other, the

whole then standing
incredibly, a shambles
magnificently held up:

or drive a huge force of
argument through the
parties' exceptional manglings

till hardly a quibble
remains whole: let
the quibble speak.

Coming Round

Ships turn into lows
they can't outrun,

the concision of the oncoming
a holding rightness, and

tigers evade into threadlike
trails till

evasion snaps shut
then turn straight

to the bothering center:
but I run on

ruffling the periphery,
the treadmill's outwheel,

declining center
or any loss of it

and no longer
crying help.

Dismantlings

Snow holds two
feet deep on
top of the big
round yew,
providing underneath
a dome for
cold-lean birds:
and even when,
the bush stirred
by kicked-up
gusts,
the dome cracks
into floats,
showboats,
the birds hang
around the slow
of the passing there.

Down Low

Snowstorms high-traveling,
furry clouds blur over
our zero air:
wind steams (or
smokes) fine snow
off the eaves, settled ghosts
trailing up and away:
the pheasant, too cold to
peck, stands on one foot
like a stiff weed.

We, We Ourselves

So nothing holds—
forget it, I already
knew it—or only
what turns and cleaves
to itself and that
is no holding in
a larger sphere—and,
anyway, nothing not
broken holds, the other
reaching across
the break to secure the missing
but at least one
hold might stay
if the other gave
way, a temporary
illusion of holding
not altogether illusory—
but then literally
nothing holds—it
does—under the
deepest fall the
rondure of the ultimate
sympathy, like
a symmetry,
turns cupping in to
the levitating explosions,
of meetings, hallelujahs,
upward drafts
afterall

Measuring Points

Squirrels in the early
spring ritual zoom, one
after the other,

winding round
the trunk and up out
over the limbs, so fast

they keep the whole
tree bobbing for
minutes: they

stop, scratch, and stop:
they get the tree as
still as their eyes.

Section

The branch sags low
this morning with
held rain:
when the squirrel,
traveling,
hits it it
dips deeply but,
shower and squirrel
lost, woofs back
way higher than it
was, a risen road
righted thru trees—
a squirrel's spent trail

Buttermilk Falls

The falls slopes and a thousand
shale notches
and inch-ledge spills
mix the water white—
so much speech of a kind,
so much to listen to,
differentials of tone and ruffle
a roiled continuum:
I sit down, draw a clear line
to disinterested attention,
my white sheets &
markers out, and
begin to take it all down.

Spring Vacation

This snow's
swayed and busted open

the fine-fingered
bushes,

Lord, leaned over
break-neck spindly yews,

put mound
bloom on the spirea,

starved the pheasant
fence-skinny,

done us all
in with flu,

and's still
coming down:

clouds, sweep out:
sky, break up:

give us some way to get
to somewhere to go.

Meeting Place

The water nearing the ledge leans down with
grooved speed at the spill then,
quickly groundless in air, bends

its flat bottom plates up for the circular
but crashes into irregularities of lower
ledge, then breaks into the white

bluffs of warped lace in free fall that
breaking with acceleration against air
unweave billowing string-maze

floats: then the splintery regathering
on the surface below where imbalances
form new currents to wind the water

away: the wind acts in these shapes, too,
and in many more, as the falls also does in
many more, some actions haphazardly

unfolding, some central and accountably
essential: are they, those actions,
indifferent, nevertheless

ancestral: when I call out to them
as to flowing bones in my naked self, is my
address attribution's burden and abuse: of course

not, they're unchanged, unaffected: but have I
fouled their real nature for myself
by wrenching their

meaning, if any, to destinations of my own
forming: by the gladness in the recognition
as I lean into the swerves and become

multiple and dull in the mists' dreams, I know
instruction is underway, an
answering is calling me, bidding me rise, or is

giving me figures visible to summon
the deep-lying fathers from myself,
the spirits, feelings howling, appearing there.